The Taxi Chronicles

(Based On a True Story)

Kerry Edwards

Table of Contents

Dedication

I would like to dedicate this story to all the people that suffered through the recession of 2008. A time that many have forgotten. Many had to find a way to get through it all the best they could. I hope this story about one person's struggle and redemption will bring hope to all the next times we are challenged.

Acknowledgments

I would like to acknowledge my family, of course, that had to put up with me changing personalities all the time and sometimes bring the personalities home.

About the Author

Kerry is a divorced father of two great children and two understanding sisters. He is a shy artist that has a great eye for observation, something that all good artists need to convey their ideas. Being so shy, he had to develop characters from TV and movies to cope with interacting with the public. As a result, he never really knew who the real Kerry was until the recession of 2008, which forced him to drive a Taxi to make ends meet. With the help of some unexpected characters, he found himself.

Prologue

The night air is humid, and it feels like it is going to rain. I am in a dark alley hiding behind a smelly dumpster with a black woman and two little kids crouching beside me. I tell the mother, "Stay calm and keep the little ones quiet." I hear shouting and screaming as someone runs by. I look back at the family, and their eyes are as big as saucers, and tears are running down their frightened faces. What the hell am I doing here? I am a sixty-year-old salesman that happens to be driving a taxi because the economy is so bad. As I sit here wondering what will happen next, my mind drifts to how all this started.

Chapter One

It was the fall of 2008, and the business I had worked with for ten years had fallen on hard times and had closed its doors. Here I was, an older man trying to find a job when the country was reeling from the recession. Sales were not the profession to be in when nobody wanted to buy. I sent resumes everywhere and applied for all kinds of jobs. The American businesses had me and would only hire part-time, so they did not have to give you insurance. They also paid you crap money as an independent contractor, so you had to handle your own taxes.

I had been a bartender for twenty years before getting into sales. It was fun, and I got to meet lots of interesting people, but I did not make enough money for the lifestyle I wanted, so I got into sales. The economy, the way it was, forced me back into bartending, which I learned, was a young man's game. My legs ached, and I couldn't remember old drinks and could not make the new ones, and of course, there was the generation gap. I just could not hack it. I sat back and took a good look at myself, and tried to see what things I could do to earn a buck.

Looking for a job was not that easy. I had to factor in my few disabilities that prevent me from getting normal jobs. I suffer from Borderline Personality Disorder. They call it that because it borders on social anxiety, depression, mania, and

ADHD, plus a host of other mental problems. All these create a world of maddening racing thoughts that make me be the most confident person one moment and a shy introvert the next. When I feel good, I can do anything. When I am shy, I have to force myself to be another person to get the job done, in other words, I become an actor. I mostly act like someone I have seen in the movies or television. It is a world that I can create in an instant. When someone is rude or pushy, I become like a John Wayne character. If a laugh is needed, I morph Jim Carrey, and I can stay in character as long as I want. Sometimes the character takes me over, and I find it difficult to go back to shy me. After years of doing this, I don't have to think about it, it just happens. They are always there when I need them. Sometimes I meet women in character, and they want me to be that way all the time. You can see the problems.

With my mental issues, and little experience other than sales or bartending, I went looking for work. One day I saw this ad in the newspaper that Taxi drivers were needed for hire. No experience necessary. The money sounded okay, and I was desperate. The only thing I knew about being a cab driver was a few trips I had taken and what I saw in the movies. Nothing could prepare me for what lay ahead.

I applied and got hired, had three days of training, then was set free. I was in the shy mode and had to decide who I was going to be to tackle this job. I was not quite sure who I was going to be until I got to class and saw what I was up against. There were twelve people in the class.

I was the only white person there, and the rest were Haitian, Black, and Latin, smelly and loud. I built a character that was bold, confident, and happy-go-lucky. Someone that people would want to get in the cab with. I would tell jokes and be a tour guide at the same time. If people liked you, they would tip you better, get your card, and use you all the time. Most of the cabbies dressed slovenly, so I decided to wear a Panama hat and flowered shirt. This would set me apart from everyone and fit the character I had created. It was my uniform.

At first, the drivers made fun of me. When they made jokes about me, I smiled or laughed and went about my business. The same ones who made fun of me actually started wearing flowered shirts. The others would cut in front of you in line when you were checking in. Some of the cocky ones would stare right at you, daring you to start something with all their friends standing around. Knowing you wouldn't make any such moves because you are outnumbered.

One morning as I was checking in, this Haitian guy came out of nowhere and cut in front of me. I grabbed him and pushed him aside, and said, "I was here first." He pushed back, and the next thing you know, people were pulling us apart. I was called into the manager's office to talk about the incident. I told him what happened, and he showed me on camera that I had touched him first, and even if I was right, I was not allowed to physically touch him. I said, "They do it all the time, and if you are running late, you could get fined." I also said, "They only do it to white cabbies, and they stick up for each other." He said, "Too bad, that's just the way it is around here. Either you deal with it or leave."

I was told to go home. He did not care if I was right or even if I was the best cabbie in the world. He just did his job and went home. I realized that this incident with the Haitian was out of character for me… or was it, I wondered.

When the manager showed me the videotape, I was amazed at what I saw. The instant before the pushing started, my body straightened up, my eyes squinted, and the voice that came out of me sounded like Clint Eastwood. I did not even think about it, it just happened. I did not plan to be Clint Eastwood and get into a pushing match. It just happened by itself. Prior to this, I hadn't even practiced fighting. I was not the sort of person who would pick fights on streets.It was something deep inside of me that was there when I needed it. Could he come to my aide when I needed him, or was he going to get me in trouble?

Being in contact with many strangers every day became very

stressful. There were people from all walks of life, and it was up to me to make their few minutes with me their best moments of the day. As a salesman, I could look in a person's eyes and see what kind of mood they were in, and I would create a character to fit the moment. For instance, ninety-five percent of New Yorkers are very demanding and critical, very nice, mind you, but critical. If I was my normal nice guy, they would chew me up and spit me out. I would become George Carlin with a slight New York accent and would be forced to play along with them and make them laugh. Throughout the day and night, I could become five or six characters. By the end of my shift, I was very tired of going in and out of personalities, and when I was extra tired, I could not get out of my last character and would take him home. When I woke up the next morning, I was back to my normal shy self. I never worried about coming out of character because things always went back to normal. From now on, I will call him Ed to make things easier to follow.

Ed had a call to a neighborhood that was supposedly off-limits to white cabbies, but I needed the money very badly and decided to go. It turned out to be a young black mother with two kids, one five years old and the other about two, in a stroller. She was surprised to see an old white cabbie but was pleased nonetheless. Her name was Ella and only had to go fifteen blocks to her boyfriend's house. The good news was it was still light out, but the bad news was

I was heading deeper into a suspicious neighborhood.

In those few minutes I talked to her, I found she was quite intelligent, had a good job, and seemed to care a great deal about her children. When I dropped her off, she asked for my card and if I would be able to pick her up in a couple of hours. I said if I did not have a fare, I would come and get her. She also told me I was the nicest Taxi driver she ever had.

The next hour or so, I had a fare or two and was thinking about Ella and if I would go back into that neighborhood at night. Before I had a chance to really think about it, she called and asked me to come and get her. She said she had an argument with her boyfriend and had to leave quickly. Without thinking much, which in hindsight was incredibly naïve of me, I said I would be there in a few minutes. When I came around the corner, it was pitch black, and she and her kids were on the curb waiting for me. I looked around to see if there was any trouble, then got out and opened the doors, helped them in then got the hell out of there.

I looked in my rearview mirror to see she was crying and asked if she was alright. She just nodded slowly. We got back to her place, and I realized it was darker here than any place I had ever been to. All the streetlights were shot out. This was no place to be at night, but I felt obligated to walk her to her door. It's just the way I was brought up. This woman and her kids were getting inside the apartment safely at my watch.

Her place was about forty or fifty yards from my cab, so I locked the doors and headed out. We got to her door, and she was trying to find the keys when all of a sudden, this crazy screaming came from the streets. It was her boyfriend and a couple of other guys. Ella started shaking and said, "He's real mean and has a bad temper. That's why I left him tonight." In the meantime, she could not find her keys. *Oh great! What the fuck am I supposed to do now?* I wondered. Well, I didn't think, I just grabbed them and ran. We ended up behind a smelly dumpster.

My thoughts were racing. I was panicking and thought I was about to be killed when all of a sudden, this strange feeling came over me. I wasn't scared anymore. My body stiffened, eyes squinted, and in a gruff voice, I told Ella, "Stay down, I'll take care of this." I had become the Clint Eastwood character again. I did not even have to think. It just happened. I looked around for some kind of weapon and found a broken baseball bat. It was perfect for kicking some ass. I reached over and picked up some dirt and rubbed it into my hands like I was getting ready to hit a home run. I was ready for those sons of bitches.

I stood up and walked out from behind the dumpster, looked in their direction, and yelled, "You looking for Ella?" The three of them just stood there with their mouths open then started walking towards me. Two of them pulled out knives. No guns? This was going to be fun. All of a sudden, they started running at me, at which time I ran towards them. I hit the first guy on the arm and felt bones cracking. Then swung at the second one and hit him squarely in the head. The third just stopped in his tracks. I said, "You fuckers had enough? I don't know which one of you is Ella's boyfriend, but I would advise you to leave her alone. If you don't, remember I know where you live, and you don't want some crazy old white dude to come over when you don't expect it and kick your ass." Now that's a lot of words coming out of my mouth, and I had no control of it. Clint was in full form. To my surprise, the guys just got up and hauled butt. This character that had jumped out of me in time had actually saved our asses. It would be safe to say that my earlier reservations were unfounded.

I gathered Ella and her kids, got them into her place, and told her if he ever messed with her again, she should call me. The look on her face was complete astonishment. I walked slowly back to my cab, just hoping someone would mess with me. Ed was nowhere to be found. Clint was driving this cab.

Slowly my mind drifted back to being Ed, and I was trying to make heads or tails of what happened. I knew I was the one that did all that crazy shit. I started shaking from head to toe and had to pull off the road just to catch my breath.

What the hell happened? Then words spilled out of my mouth, "Aren't you going to thank me?" It was Clint's voice. I was actually two people at the same time. I could hear his voice and respond to it. "What happened back there?" I said, "You just appeared out of nowhere. You took me over without me thinking about it. How is that possible?" "Ed, my friend," he said, "You were about to totally freak out back there, so I guess your mind called me to help you out." "But I could have been killed by what you did," I screamed. "Yeah, but you had a better chance of getting hurt if you did nothing," Clint said in a confident fatherly voice. So I replied, "Are you always going to be consciously in my head, or am I going to get some peace and quiet from you?" "You haven't thanked me yet for saving your ass." Clint murmured, "Okay, Okay, thank you," I said. "About your question, I'll be here whenever you need me," Clint said, then laughed. "What does that mean?" I asked him. There was no answer. "Talk to me," I yelled.

But there was complete silence.

Well, I guess I didn't need him right then. *This is great,* I thought. *I am sitting on the side of the road, talking to myself in two different voices.* I had better get back to work and let things take care of themselves. So that's what I did. I went home.

The next few days seemed normal to me. I slipped in and out of character to meet my customers' needs, and there were not any stressful fares, so Clint never made an appearance which was a great relief to me. You can't imagine what it felt like waiting for this personality to pop up and create a dangerous situation I couldn't get out of. Well, at least I had only one subliminal character to worry about.

Let me explain a few things for people that have never driven a taxi in Orlando. You rent the cab from the company for $125.00 for a twelve-hour shift. My shift was from 10 am to 10 pm, and every fare you get goes towards that $125. Everything over that is what you take home minus the gas you have to pay. Some nights I would go home owing them money, but through the week, I would take home about $70.00 a night. That is why I had to take every fare they sent me, no matter where it was. I had to make money. I had to pay rent. I had to eat, simple as that.

Inside your cab is a computer that tracks where you are in the city. The city is made up of forty grids about one mile by one mile. If you are in that grid and someone calls for a ride in that grid, your computer will let you know that a call is coming and tell you if other cabs are in the area that have gotten in the grid before you, therefore they will get the call before you. They can turn it down or take it. If you take it, you must go and pick up that fare no matter what unless your life is in danger. Then you have to call the dispatcher and tell the reasons why you are not going to pick up the fare. As I mentioned before, I took every fare no matter where it was or how bad I thought it was going to be. There are certain incidents and strange characters you meet when you take every fare that sometimes you get surprised.

One night I had a call to a small apartment complex. The name and address came across my dashboard, so I went there to get my fare. The thing about apartments is that sometimes it's hard to find the number, which is what happened this night.

I got out of my cab and started looking, but for the life of me, I could not find the place. I heard some music coming from down the hall so I decided to go there and ask if they could help me. The door was open, so I popped my head in and asked if they knew where 1701–G was, and by George, they said, "Right here."

It so happened that it was a bachelorette party, and they were not expecting me so soon. They screamed, "Come on in and party with us." Now you have to realize a few things. There were five girls, all in their late twenties, all good-looking and drunk, asking me, an old man, to party with them. My mind went into overdrive. Did they really mean it? Did they want me to drink with them, have sex, dance, or what?

I stood there and could not speak for about thirty seconds when all of a sudden, my Scottish, Sean Connery accent came out, and of course, his cool James Bond personality followed. The girls loved it, and I again could not control this character.

I had a few drinks, danced a little, and just blew these girls away. It was any man's dream. Five young girls, all fighting for my affection. Ed was in Sean's head trying to tell him of all the rules he was breaking, but Sean was driving this cab.

Finally, thirty minutes later, one of the girls said they had reservations at a restaurant and had to go. As we were heading to the cab, all the girls had to stop and take a picture with me. They called me the coolest cabbie they ever had and begged me to party on at the restaurant. Having a drink and dancing back at their apartment could be covered up before I checked out but being in a public place was a no-no, even Sean knew that.

I told them I could lose my job. I took them to the restaurant and charmed the hell out of them on the way. When I dropped them off, one of them was actually crying that I couldn't join them. Sean's head was so big he could hardly get out of the cab. Ed was there along for the ride waiting for all this to end, waiting to gain control. The cab drove away with a phone number or two and pulled off the side of the road again to figure this shit out.

I sat there realizing I had lost control again when all of a sudden Sean said in his finest Scottish brogue, "Well, sonny, did ya have a good time?" I screamed, "You just can't come out of nowhere and take me over. It's not right." Again Sean said, "DID YOU HAVE A GOOD TIME?" I said, "No, but I think YOU did. I was worried about getting in trouble and all that crap." Well, actually, near the end, I started to let go and enjoy the situation. No matter who was in control, I was still in the company of five girls that were enjoying me, Sean, or whoever it was. Even I couldn't deny it was fun to be the center of attention of five beautiful women.

I was trying to put all this on the table and find out why I was doing this. I know I have mental problems, but I take medication that is supposed to keep me leveled. The situation reminded me of the movie "Me myself and Irene" starring Jim Carrey. His character had personality issues that came out with stress, but as long as he took his meds, he was okay. That was a movie, but this, my life, was real. I can only imagine if I did not take my pills. I could be totally whacked.

I decided to see a phycologist, and he said that since I had a rocky childhood and no father figure, I would reach out to anyone that made me feel comfortable, and those guys were found on TV and in movies. My parents used the television as a babysitter, so I would spend hours in front of the tube and really thought what I saw was real. I had no one to tell me different. He said I may even have more characters come out, mostly in the time of stress.

I remember when I was seven, I climbed up on the roof, pretended to be Superman, and thought that since he could fly, so could I. I ended up in the bushes with a broken arm a split lip and could not figure out what I did wrong. As I got older, I would pretend to be all different characters and would practice their facial expressions in the mirror. That is how I came to have a repertoire of personalities that I could call on. The difference was I was always in control. I can understand how my subconscious would create these guys, but not being able to stop them has been scary. If I would go to a doctor and tell him about this, he may keep me from work, and I needed the money. So I guessed I will have to deal with it for now and take it one day at a time.

The more I worked, the less tolerance I had for asshole customers. One day I was at a hotel waiting for a fare when this guy started waving at me like he was upset at something, so I pulled up to him. "It's about time," he screamed. Now that is not the way to start anything, especially when the man you're yelling at is going to have your life in his hands.

I got out of my cab to open the door when I realized we had a problem. This man was at least four hundred pounds and, in my opinion, could not fit in my taxi comfortably. I said, "Excuse me, sir, I believe you would be more comfortable in a van." Which was a polite way of saying, "I don't want your smelly, sweaty fat ass in my cab." Not a nice thing to think, but that was the way I was feeling that morning. "I am in a hurry," he retorted. "I ride in vehicles this size all the time" "Okay, sir, let's have a go at it," I said. Plus, I was curious to see how he was going to squeeze into the front seat. I thought I could push the seat back and give him a fighting chance. He would have none of it.

"I always sit in the back," he demanded. Now, this guy is getting to me, and none of my characters have shown up yet, and that made me a little nervous. I walked up to the back door, opened it and stood back, and watched. What I saw next was truly amazing. This behemoth of a man pushed, shoved, and packed his body in my back seat. The springs on the cab groaned. When he was in, the whole right side of my cab was almost touching the ground. The driver's side was almost off the ground and was truly a sight to behold. It was like putting ten pounds of shit in a five-pound bag.

I climbed in, and off we went. It sounds like I don't like fat people, but that is not true. It just seems I run into the ones that have this overbearing attitude that they are better than you, plus the fact this one truly did have a unique odor and did sweat entirely too much.

I was polite and professional and asked his name – which he would not give – but just barked out an address and said, "Hurry." As I drove, I heard him ask, "What time is it?" I said, "10:15," and he rudely said, "I wasn't talking to you. I am on the phone." I could swear he did not have a cell phone. As I looked closer, I could see he was wearing a Bluetooth hearing device in his ear.

Just another thing that bothers me is people who wear these and look like they are talking to themselves, and you can't tell if they are talking to you. I could feel Clint stirring in my head. I was doing a good job keeping him in line, but I could not keep him down for long. I had better step on it and get this guy to his destination.

I heard him say, "Where's a good place for dinner?" I ignored him because I thought he was still speaking on the Bluetooth. "Where is a good place for steak?" he shouted. I looked in the rearview mirror to see he was staring at me. I said in my friendly Ed voice, "I thought you were still on the phone. Umm, a nice place to eat near to where you're going is the Outback restaurant." Then he asked, "Is it this hot here all the time?" I said, "No, the winters are great. Very little humidity," He said, "I am not talking to you. I am on the phone." That was the straw that broke the camel's back. My body tightened up, and Clint came flying out of my mouth. "Listen, fat-man-who-won't-give-his-name, you either talk to me or talk on the phone, you can't do both in this cab, and if you don't start treating me with respect, I'll drop you off at the nearest salad bar." His jaw dropped past his three chins, and his face turned bright red. "I can have your job for saying that," he said. Then it was silent for what seemed an eternity. Ed was doing all he could to keep Clint from saying anything else when all of a sudden, the fat man's face went back to normal, and a big smile flashed across his giant face, and he started laughing. "That's great," he said. "That's fucking unbelievable. No cabbie ever told me off before, and I know I can be an asshole. My name is Charles," he said. "Sorry I was such a jerk. What was your name again?" I looked him right in the eyes and said, "Clint." He looked at me, then at my badge that said Ed, then looked back at me again and said, "Nickname?" I said, "Yea, nickname." This guy gets off the phone and becomes somewhat of a decent person. We have a little small talk, and I drop him off at his place, and to my surprise, he gives me a huge tip. So the lesson to learn from this was that it is better not to take any shit from anyone than be nice to those who are being assholes to you.

There was always a lot of downtime with plenty of time to think. I tried to analyze myself and figure out why these guys came out of nowhere without my practicing with them. I started researching all types of disorders, mental problems, and syndromes. Anything to get a sniff of why I was doing what I was doing, nothing was making sense. I took another avenue and started studying memory, how we remember items, and how long they are stored in the brain. After several months, I came up with an interesting theory.

Just before I started driving a taxi, I was playing golf. It was April, and the weather was starting to get hot. Thunderstorms were always a threat, even in April when the cold air from the north hits the hot air from the south and creates hail, wind, thunder, and lightning. Usually, you can hear it coming or see the dark clouds. That day there wasn't a cloud in the sky with a bit of wind from the south.

I was playing pretty well and was having a great time. I was playing the last hole and hit my second shot to the green. I pulled my cart up to the green and got my putter out of the bag, and started walking to my ball. Now, within a nanosecond, several things happened. The hair raised on the back of my neck and arms. My putter started to vibrate, then flew out of my hand toward a palm tree about ten feet from me. Then WHAM, lightning strikes the tree.

The next thing I remember is hearing sirens. I open my eyes and realize I am in the back of an ambulance with all kinds of activities. Once they saw I was conscious, one asked how I was feeling. I really could not give him an answer. All I knew was my life had changed.

I wasn't struck by lightning but close enough to have a lot of volts go through me. The doctors checked me out and said I could have been killed, but I was fine and was released. It was one of those storms where the hot air is in front of the cold air, causing friction, and the lightning is usually out front giving no warning. As I mentioned, I checked out fine, but something was different. I seemed to remember everything that happened to me in my entire life, and I could read and memorize anything in a split second. At this time, I did not know how to utilize this or if I even wanted to. I was okay but felt strange

I realized that after that, it was easier to get into character, even some that I had never done before. Staying in character and not having control when driving bothered me, but I had to deal with it the best I could. The lightning strike definitely had something to do with it.

I was on the internet and had heard about somebody coming out of a coma speaking a foreign language. I researched it because I found it interesting that it is very rare. Maybe ten people in the world have this. All are hit in the head or have had a stroke or have mental distress, but none are struck by a bolt from Zeus.

I started doing more research. The brain remembers and stores everything it sees. It only uses what is necessary to carry on daily life. If you could pull out memories easily, your brain would be flooded, and you would go mad.

It stores long-term memories all over your brain. These people that woke up with a foreign language had actually heard it in their life and were brought to the surface with head trauma or psychogenic injuries or maladies, not electricity, but nobody had an instant recall.

Now we are getting somewhere. All those characters that I saw one time or another in my life had made an impression on me seemed to appear easily after my electric shock. Clint Eastwood, on the other hand, is another story. He appears and takes control of me, thinking he is indestructible. The problem is, I like that feeling when I am him, whether I complain about it or not. This is just my theory right now. I didn't want to go to a doctor because they would put me in the hospital, and I could not pay my bills. Money is a bitch.

Chapter Two

As time went on, I found that I had the ability to dig down and pull these characters out. The point I am getting to is I can watch these characters on the screen and get emotionally attached to them. They can be brought to the surface because my brain thinks they are necessary for survival at a moment's notice. I have watched them, and since I can remember everything, I can conjure up an exact replica of how I perceive him but forgetting it is just an actor playing a part and because he wasn't hurt on-screen sets me up for dangerous situations in real life. It is pretty fascinating that my characters have no fears whatsoever.

I would have many, many characters as customers. Two that I was fond of were Jack and Charley. They were World War II vets that had been friends for sixty years and had joined the Army simultaneously.

I had a call one night for a pick-up at a bar downtown and pulled up and beeped my horn. I saw two old men staggering towards me, laughing their asses off. I got out of my cab to open the door for them, and they both fell down, still laughing. While I was helping them up, three young punks jumped in my cab ahead of them. I told them that this cab was spoken for and to get out, at which time they got out, came towards me screaming and said they were going to kick my ass

Before I had time to react or have Clint help, these two eighty-year-old vets jumped on them and beat the shit out of them. It was great and was over in about thirty seconds. Jack and Charley climbed in, and off we went. They lived in a retirement home about five minutes away. They asked for my card, and every Thursday night at the same time, I picked them up and drove them home. And every time, they had a Great War story for me.

One afternoon I had a call to a suspect neighborhood and had to talk myself into going there. Money is a powerful motivator that sent me into the hood. I found the address and said to myself, "Here we go again."

The house was run down, and on the porch were five or six women all dressed up and had on perfume that I could smell from the street. While I was looking at them, this big black man comes around the house and walks to the cab. He weighs about three hundred pounds, has on a dirty white tee-shirt, very dirty pants, and no shoes. There is a hole in his throat from an operation, and he has to speak with one of those talking devices. I swear this is true.

I take my job seriously and try to treat everyone the same. I get out and open the door, and this smell of urine fills the air. I am in my Ed mode, and I think I can handle this. Not sure, but I think so. I reach out my hand and say, "My name is Ed, and I will be your driver today." This big smelly behemoth of a man looks at me and starts laughing. It's one of that down-on-one-knee kind of laugh. I am staring at him, and he is beginning to sweat profusely. Then this crap starts coming out of the hole in his neck. I am thinking, "Do any of the cabbies go through this, or is it just me?"

I reach in my cab and give him some tissues to clean himself, and he just throws them on the ground. It is the turning point of the fare. He had been rude, and I had the right to turn him away. Just then, I heard Clint and Sean say, "Go ahead, we have your back," and I screamed, "Yeah, but I have to do this." In a mechanical voice, the big guy says, "Are you screaming at me?" and I said, "No, I was just clearing my throat," which he thought was funny and gave me a high five.

He finally gets in the car and tells me he has to go to the bank around the corner to get cash to pay his hoes. I said, "What?" He says, "Hoes, hoes, I gots to pay my hoes." I looked at him then on the porch and said, "Whores?" he said, "Yea, hoes." We drive around the block, go to an ATM, and are back in five minutes. I thought, "All this for a $3.00 fare," but the ride was not over. He gave me a $50.00 tip and said, "Give me your card. You have class, and I want you to drive my girls around." I am sitting there smelling this guy and blurt out, "I need $300.00 a day." He said, "Done, plus tips and all the sex you want." I gave him a card and wrote down a wrong number, and got the hell out of there. I again had to pull off the side of the road and laugh as I had never laughed before. It was funny because, for a split second, I almost gave him my actual phone number. Yes, as bad as that was, some dark place deep down inside wanted to play out that game

I have found that most people that ride in taxies don't have a license. That is usually because of a DUI, or they can't afford a car. Many customers are drunk and don't want to drive. I guess a cross-section of weird characters can come out of them. In Orlando, tourists will make up half my fares.

It was mid-day, and I was cruising the convention center hoping to pick up a stray fare and saw a man waving me down. He looked normal, middle-aged, clean, and had some class. Not like the fares I have had lately, and I could use normal today.

His name was Dr. Stein, and he was a dentist from Chicago. I asked him where he wanted to go, and he looked around like he was being watched and whispered, "Can you take me to some dancing girls." I said, "Sure," and off we went. It was about 12:30 pm. I dropped him off, gave him my card, and told him to call me when he wanted a ride back to his hotel. I got a call three hours later, and it was Dr. Stein screaming incoherently to come and pick him up. I got there in about fifteen minutes and drove up to find him lying in the parking lot, passed out. I went over to him, shoved him in the back of the cab, and took off. I pulled into a quiet place so I could get a handle on this.

I turned around and looked at him. His eyes were wide open, his hair was messed up, and he was stone drunk. I said, "Doc, what's the matter?" "I spent $2,000.00 on those bitches." he whined, "And I want to kill myself." "Okay, calm down, and let's talk about this." My mind went into overdrive, and I tried not to panic. It's not every day someone wants to off himself right in front of you. I said, "Doc, it's only money. You don't need to have those thoughts over frigging money." he moans, "I had $1,500.00 in cash, and they made me go to the ATM and get more. They used me. Everybody uses me. I want to kill myself." At this time, he pulls out a green knife-like object and tries to cut his wrists. I jump back there and take it away from him, and he starts crying like a baby and passes out.

Clint and Sean are not even in my mind. I react on some weird instinct. I mean, we are not taught what to do when something like this happens. I decided to go through his wallet and found a card for a physiatrist in Chicago and gave him a call. I tell his secretary the situation and Dr. Albright comes to the phone. "Hello, How can I be of help?" he says. All the tension and anxiety I have quickly goes away, and I chuckle under my breath. Yes chuckle. This guy sounds exactly like Jerry Lewis in the movie Nutty Professor, my favorite character of all time. Humor does have a way to disarm situations sometimes, and this certainly is one of those.

I take a quick thirty seconds to give the doctor the run-down. I said, "Doctor, if he is your patient, what's he doing here in Florida?" He said, "Do you see the light-colored scars on his arm? Those are the ones from the dull green knife, making marks for attention. The darker scar tissues are from the red knife that put him in the hospital twice."

He told me that he had some financial problems but was on medication that was keeping him stable, and he really wanted to go on this trip. "What is your name?" he asked. "Ed," I said. "Okay, Ed, listen to me very carefully and do exactly what I say. I want you to take your forefinger and middle finger and tap him on his forehead, right between the eyes, for about thirty seconds. After this, he will wake up with no recollection of what happened, and I must not be on the phone. This is a post-hypnotic suggestion with a tapping solution and should last until you get him to a hospital." I did as he said. Dr. Stein woke up feeling nauseous with no memory of what happened.

I take him to the emergency room and give them the low down. They whisk him away, and I don't even get paid. As long as he is alright, I think. The next day I got a call from

Dr. Albright thanking me for helping and thanking the Lord he did not have the red knife.

Some of my customers are beautiful women, and if you don't watch out, you can get involved with them. One morning I picked up an attractive girl about thirty-five, and she was crying (I'm a sucker for tears). When I say attractive, I mean wow! Clint, Sean, and Ed werespeechless. She said, "Take me to the nearest pet shelter. My cat ran away last night, and I need another one." Since Ed was driving this cab and he wanted to please everyone, especially the pretty ones, he gave her the full treatment. He tried to stop the tears, make her laugh, and we went and got her a new cat. Clint and Sean were staying out of this one. As a matter of fact, they were sitting in the back of Ed's brain, watching him fumble all over himself.

It's a funny thing about fumbling. Some people find it annoying, and others find it cute. Kara found it cute. That's her name, Kara from Minnesota, and of course, she is a high-maintenance topless dancer with a father complex. It's the only thing I could think of. Don't get me wrong, I'm a fairly good-looking guy for my age, but she is far out of my league.

We went to get her a new cat, and as a matter of fact, I helped her pick it out (she liked that) then headed back to her apartment, which was a $20 fare. She paid me and leaned over, thanked me, gave me a kiss on the cheek. Then asked for my card. She said, "I call for taxies all the time, and most of the cabbies are scumbags or can't speak English. You are the first nice driver I've had in a very long time. Could you be my driver every time I need you? I will pay you well."

My life flashed before me. Everything said run, run away as fast as you can and don't look back. "Just call me," I blurted out. "Call me anytime," I said as I fumbled for the car keys. I neverthought I would see her again, but I got a call from her about 11 am the very next day. "Hi Ed, you handsome thing, can you pick me up at 12 and take me to work? I was twenty miles away but said, "Sure, see you soon." I was in it now. I knew I wouldn't make that much money, but I would see a beautiful woman that smelled wonderful.

When I dropped her off, she asked if I could pick her up at 6 pm, and of course, I said yes. This would be the routine for the next few weeks. I would take her to work, pick her up three to four times a week, and then fantasize about being with her for hours.

Then it happened. I was dropping her off at about 6:30 one night when she looked me square in the eyes and said, "Do you want to come in?" My legs got weak, and I felt like all blood was draining out of my body. I was screaming silently for Clint or Sean to appear and give me some help but just heard two faint voices say, "You don't need our help, boy, you need some Viagra." I just chuckled under my breath and followed her in.

I was taking a big chance doing this, but to hell with it. This is just a lousy taxi job, and she was giving me all the signs. We got into her apartment, and I had to hold my breath to keep from hyperventilating and passing out. It was great. She made no bones about it. She said, "I'm horny and want to have sex." I must tell you I was quite proud of myself. I handled myself very well for my age. I felt twenty years younger and had a skip in my step. When I was leaving, I remembered I forgot to ask her for the fare and decided it was worth it. This went on for about three weeks, me taking her to and from work four times a week and having sex twice a week. I could not bring myself to charge her for her rides

In reality, she was giving me sex for taxi rides, and I was not complaining. It was a matter-of-fact relationship. Having sex with no questions was a man's dream until I committed the first deadly sin of sex on the side. I wanted it to become personal, I wanted to know more about her, and I wanted to spend time with her.

I said, "Kara, you are off tomorrow. Do you want to have dinner? She hesitated then said, "Yes, pick me up at 7:30." The next day I was all excited about my date with Kara. I washed my truck, got a haircut, and was at her doorstep at exactly 7:30. I knocked on the door, no answer. I knocked again, but this time heard some sounds coming from inside her apartment. I listened closely, and my heart dropped to the floor. They were sex sounds, screams, and moans. That bitch. She knew I would be here at this time and was putting on a show for me. She was telling me she was in charge of her sex life, and I was literally along for the taxi ride. I left there, feeling hurt and sorry for myself. I let my truck take me wherever it wanted to go.

I ended up at the beach and decided to stop, have a few beers and drown my sorrows. The place was a dive right on the ocean, perfect for how I felt. When I walked in, it was about 8:30 and starting to fill up. I managed to find a spot at the bar and just ordered a beer when I heard this female voice behind me say, "Hey sweetie, you look like you can use some company?" I was staring down into my beer, thinking it may be nice to talk to someone, and turned to see who was attached to this soothing voice. Nothing prepared me for what I saw.

Here stood an eighty-year-old woman with blue eye shadow, too many layers of makeup, red lipstick that was smeared, and way too much perfume. I was not shocked because this place was filling up with older strange-looking people. She had a nice smile, so I asked her to sit down. The mood I was in, any company was good company.

As we started to talk, I noticed she had very young

and lively eyes, which made me feel better, but I was down, really down. Her name was Mable which fit perfectly. I found myself talking about Kara and all the things that had happened. After a few beers, I actually started to relax but was sure nothing could get me out of this funk.

There was a little activity behind me, so I turned around to see what was going on. There was this small stage, and a strange, old, biker-looking dude was about to say something into the microphone. "Hello, ladies and gentlemen, welcome to our weekly Karaoke contest." I looked around to see all types of people preparing themselves for their turn at the mic.

Most of them were in their fifties and sixties, dressed like beach people, and basically looked worn out. Many of them had tattoos, and some had teeth missing. All of them had their own CDs, which I thought was weird. I was feeling even more depressed, and I just knew this night was going to be a downer.

The MC introduced the first contestant, an older woman dressed in 60's attire. I could not watch and turned around to drink my beer. The music started. It was somewhere over the rainbow. I squinted my eyes, waiting for the first sour note but instead heard this fantastic voice that was dead on for Judy Garland. I swung around to see this strange woman performing with class and professionalism. Was I in the twilight zone? Something was not right. The voice did not match the woman.

The next contestant got up, an elderly gent with just a swimming suit. He banged out Elvis Presley, as good as I have ever heard. Three more people performed, one better than the next. As I sat there taking all this in, I realized I was not depressed anymore. All this fantastic entertainment was making me feel great. Even Mabel was starting to look good. Still, how could all this talent be here in the same place?

It turns out all these people live in a small trailer park just behind this bar, and fate had brought them together. As a matter of fact, they travel from one karaoke contest to another, pooling the winnings. It helps them supplement their social security. I guess fate brought me here to this bar. I walked in hours ago in a terrible mood, and I was leaving feeling great, with Kara a faded memory.

Chapter Three

We are all looking down at a proverbial rabbit hole. At least, I know I do. I wonder what it would be like to do something totally off the cuff. Thinking about it makes my stomach go into *'Devils Triangle'*. The area from your left shoulder to your right shoulder, then down to your navel and back up to your left shoulder. This is the place that aches when you have a broken heart. This is the grieving area that takes over your mind leading you to pray for it to go away.

I know this to be true, and yet I still want to peer down that rabbit hole. It had been a week since Clint or Sean added to my activities, and I missed that adrenaline rush. I was going in and out of characters to fit in with my fares, but I still missed looking down the rabbit hole. Why did I miss it? Maybe it's like going into a scary movie knowing you are going to get scared out of your mind. You might hate that feeling but yet, you can't wait for it to happen. However, this is real life, and I shouldn't be searching for that high. Nevertheless, that is exactly what I want.

I had a cup of coffee in the morning, got ready for work while I wondered what I could do to challenge myself for the day. I had been doing characters to fit different situations. Let's try something different, maybe I should pick one and try to stay in that character all day. I guess you could call it method acting. Now, all I had to do was choose a character that I could handle. I drove to a beautiful park by the water, pulled out my canvas chair, and set it up in the shade.

Shade is a wonderful thing in Florida. The wind was blowing straight at me when the temperature was about 78 degrees. The perfect time to let my mind wander and find someone in my subconscious that I could be all day long. I rummaged through movies with different personalities that would fit me, but nothing came to mind. Perhaps, I was trying too hard. I closed my eyes and let the character pick me. As soon as I closed my eyes, a man popped into my head – Denzel Washington.

I have always been a fan of his work and watched him grow as an actor. He could play any role from a meek man to a strong leader and even had some *kick-ass* in him. I liked him in 'The Book of Eli', where he was quiet and confident. When the situation arose, he defended himself quite well, and it was like watching an assassin. His big smile, the long strides that made him glide, oh yeah, this is definitely the man I'm going to emulate.

So, I watched his movies to identify the little things that were a part of his character. I practiced in front of the mirror and picked up his mannerisms quickly with my new enhanced memory. I took long strides around the house until I felt confident. This was all new to me. From my subconscious, Clint and Sean popped out from nowhere exactly when the situation called for them. This was a character being created in the process. When I felt I had nailed Denzel's character, I decided to head downtown to test him out.

Later, I pulled under a tree and got out of the car. All of a sudden, my heart started beating faster, and I could feel the moisture on my brow. It was a familiar feeling that I had before I went on stage. I felt the butterflies in my stomach and the whole nine yards. I really didn't like that feeling because I was not looking for this adrenaline rush.

When I went on stage, I would get nervous because I told myself I couldn't do well or that I would embarrass myself. Eventually, I stopped after realizing that nobody knew what I was doing. I could screw up all day, and no one would know except me. So, I calmed down and started going with the flow. I walked with long strides and flashed that big smile. I felt invincible. I figured this is the way Denzel felt about many of his characters. I was hoping someone would mess with me so I could beat the crap out of them.

I stopped dead in my track and felt sick to my stomach. I realized Denzel played a character in movies, but this was real life. I could get seriously hurt, and subsequently, I decided to stop and go back to just being me. Here's something interesting, when conscious, Ed is himself, and he knows right from wrong and acts rationally. When he gets in character, Ed acts and thinks like the character from a movie, which can be dangerous. Clint put him in some bad situations, suffice to say, one impulsive character is enough.

I better hold off being another person right now.

Around 4 pm, I was in South Orlando on this normal day, and, as usual, I had conformed myself to fit in with my passengers. An address came across my dash, should I accept it? It was on the edge of a funky neighborhood. I thought to myself, there is still light out, and I needed the money. So it's decided then, and off I went.

My GPS brought me to an address with a broken mailbox at the end of a long dirt driveway that led to a small and eerie cottage. There were several broken-down cars in the yard, and my Spidey sense told me to beware. I was at the end of the driveway looking, smelling, and tasting the situation. One thing that being a cab driver has taught me is to check everything when things don't seem right. All of a sudden, I heard someone on my left weakly mutter, *"Help me."* I looked out of the window and couldn't see anyone. Then, I heard it again *"Help me."* I searched in the direction of the voice, but this time, I looked down and found someone lying in the bushes. I jumped out of the car and walked over to the guy in a leather jacket and a pierced nose beaten to a pulp. He pissed his pants and smelled like a brewery.

I was getting ready to call the police when I heard Clint say in his fatherly voice, *"I thought I taught you better."*

"What are you talking about?" I replied.

"Well, you're going to help him, aren't you?"

"He's all beat up.", I said. *"And, he might be*

dangerous."

"Grow a pair and help the poor bastard." Clint said.

"You haven't been in my head for 2 weeks, and now you want me to help this guy? Where have you been?"

"I have been letting you work things out for yourself, and if you needed me, I would have been there for you. You have been doing pretty well."

"If I do this, I need you to have to my back."

"Don't worry. We have your back, including the new guy." Clint said. Looking back, I was too distracted to understand what he meant by that.

I walked back over to the guy, who was passed out. I checked him for weapons, but he was just carrying a wallet and credit card. He started to come back to his senses.

"Hey man, are you OK? Do you want to go to the hospital?" I asked

"What's your name?"

"My name is Ian, and I don't want to go to the hospital." declared Ian.

"Ok Ian, that's up to you, but what the hell happened to you?" I asked.

"My friend and I were drinking vodka, and all of a sudden, he jumped up and literally kicked the piss out of me. I stumbled out the door and managed to crawl here and call for a cab." He said.

"Were you doing any drugs?" I questioned because I had

to know what kind of guy I was putting in my backseat. He could hit me over the head and rob me. They don't have a partition to the back seat like other big cities.

"We were smoking some pot, doing some cocaine and vodka." says Ian.

"Well damn, is that all? That was a sure-fire cocktail for danger."

By him telling me that, I had every right not to drive him anywhere. I could have left him in the bushes, but I couldn't because he needed my help. Moreover, I didn't want Clint to give me any shit. It's not like he's going anywhere because he's in my frigging head. I also wanted to look down the rabbit hole.

I opened my trunk and looked in the handy dandy taxi kit that I put together. Paper towels and air freshener were waiting for drunks that puked in my back seat. Even though we were told not to keep any weapons, I had a nightstick for protection. There was also a gum to keep my breath fresh and a towel. I laid out the towel for him so that he didn't mess up my seat.

While I was helping him into the cab, he told me where he was going. The good news is, it was 10 blocks away. What's the bad news? It was a 5 dollar fare. As we made our way there, he asked to stop at Walgreens. As I pulled into the parking lot, I checked in, *"Are you OK to go in?"* He claimed, *"I'm feeling better, let me go in."* I walked around and opened the door to see if he staggered, but he seemed ok. I watched him for a second, and then he made a beeline to the liquor store. I tried to stop him but *"Fuck it"* Let him go where he wants and get on with the night. Five minutes later, he comes out of the store chugging a liter of Ketel One. I thought to myself, at least the guy has some class. He stood in the middle of the street with the bottle tipped up going to town. I jumped out, ran over to grab him by the arm, and managed to get him into the back seat. I jerked the bottle out of his hand, which was now half-empty and put it on the floor. I turned around to say something to him, but he was passed out and pissed his pants again.

Luckily, I remembered the address to his old two-story Motel #6. At least, this is what it used to be. This place had a chain-link fence with one way in and out. I pulled into this place which had surely seen better days. The security guard knocked on my window and asked. *"Your ride has to check-in at the front desk."* I turned around, and Ian was still unconscious, so I went inside by myself. This place had a musty smell that reminded me of my grandmother's old house. The lady behind the desk asks, *"Who are you bringing in?"*

"Ian, I don't know his last name. He's passed out."

"Ian Didler. You have a handful there." she said in a concerned tone.

"What kind of place is this?"

"The county has set this up for low-income people."

"Why is there a security guard and a high fence?"

"Well." She paused for a moment before saying, *"Most of the people in here are addicts. The police know about it, but they leave them alone as long as there is no selling to outsiders, no overdoses, and no fights. They thought it was a good idea to have them all in one place where they could keep an eye on them. Ian was a decorated Marine in Iraq who suffered from severe PTSD. Every month, he gets a check from the government, which he spends on rent and drugs.* She explains, *"The drugs are to make him forget about what happened over there."*

She gave me his room number, which was on the first floor. Thank God! So, I walked back to the cab where Ian was passed out. He was drooling with his mouth open wide. I looked at him differently now that I knew a little about Ian and what he was going through.

While driving around trying to find his room, I noticed the different people hanging outside. Drug addiction does not care about your race, religion, or any other unique characteristic. The eyes of the drug addicts were all fixated on me as I passed by. It was dark now, and the street lights were on, casting strange shadows everywhere I looked. At the side of the streets, the lights were not working but over here, the lights had to stay on so the cops could stay out.

Clothes hung on the railing, and the breeze carried the

smell of pot. All kinds of loud but not too loud music were being played; it was mostly vulgar rap. It was just loud enough to be annoying but not enough to attract the police, demanding them to turn it down. I was listening to the words while driving and could tell there was an underlying message of pain and suffering. This right here is the one thing that rap could definitely do along with the driving bass. The woofers made my windows vibrate, which was terrifying, to say the least.

I found room 107 and pulled up right in front. I remember seeing a room key on Ian when I was checking him. I went around to open the door and noticed we were drawing a crowd. I was getting a little nervous, but Clint had my back, which actually made me more anxious. Crap, that's all I need, a loud character that doesn't fear anything.

I tried to wake Ian up, but he just couldn't get his senses together. I tried lifting him out, but it was like holding a giant bag of potatoes. His weight was shifting all over the place. I looked up and saw ten unruly guys staring at me. The only way to get him in the room was with some help. I took a deep breath and asked, *"Hey guys, could I get a little help here getting him in the room."* The big guy wrapped in tattoos barked. *"Is that Ian?"* I said *"Yes"* in my most confident masculine voice. To which he replied, *Go fuck yourself."*

My mind was processing a lot of things, none of which were good. Then, the big one says, *"Yeah, We'll come down and help. That little wimp owes me some money"*. Panic shot through me as I was afraid that being myself would get my ass kicked. To make matters worse, if Clint came roaring out, I would get beat up even worse. Then, a feeling came over me; I hadn't felt this one before. Lord knows why it made me feel strangely calm and confident. I have recently learned not to think too much. Ride the horse in the direction it's going, as they say.

Out of the 10 men, 5 came down, including the big guy. With this new sense of calm, I was able to slow down and take a closer look at things. I noticed certain things about him that may help me in the future. For instance, I noticed his gang tattoos which were probably done in prison. His eyes were dilated and twitching, which pointed to the fact he was high on drugs. The other guys were marked up with the same tattoos excluding some of them that had military tattoos. They were all carrying a nightstick. Simply put, it did not look good for me, but my heart rate was running at its normal pace, and I felt oddly confident.

They came over to my taxi, surrounded me, and the big one said, *"We'll take Ian to his room. Let us take it from here."* In a voice that sounded just like Denzel Washington, I said, *"Listen guys, it is my job to make sure the passenger makes it safely into his residence, at which time I receive payment for the rendered services."* Now, I knew who the new guy Clint was talking about.

"What if we don't let you and tell you to fuck off?" The big guy screamed with spit flying everywhere. I walked away from the cab, taking long rhythmic steps in the typical Denzel Washington fashion. I paced back and forth for a few seconds eyeing the nightsticks, and said, *"Do you know who this is?"* *"Yeah, a little piece of crap that owes us money."* said a guy with a smaller physique.

"How many of you were in the military and served in Iraq?" I asked. They all acknowledged with nods, and now, I had a plan. I walked around with long strides, my arms down by my side and a serious expression on my face. I said, *"Let me tell you a few things before you make a big mistake. That man in my cab has several medals for serving in Iraq for putting his life on the line to save others which could have been any of you. He suffers from terrible PTSD and gets no help from the government but a check that I'm sure you have no trouble taking from him. Did serving cause disabilities, mental or physical?"* They all confirmed except the big guy. He just kept twitching, and the fact I was making sense to his friends made him more agitated. *"All of that may be true, but the fact is we can still make hurt you and take his money."*

I looked them all in the eye as I went on to make my case, *"Listen guys. Think about it. You are not going to hurt me. Any disturbance here will bring the police in and cause all kinds of trouble. You don't want that. Help me get Ian into his room"* I started to lean over to grab Ian's arm when the big guy said, *"You might be right about us hurting you but, fuck you. We are taking his money, and there is nothing you can do about it."*

As I tested my strategy out, I said, *"Everyone knows that anyone who served in the military is taught not to leave their fellow soldiers behind. You might as well put a bullet in his brain because he can't take care of himself right now."*

"We didn't know he served. He never talked about it." they said.

"You didn't know he served, so you took advantage of someone weaker than you." I shot back. I was walking on thin ice, and I could feel Clint getting restless, letting Denzel do his thing diplomatically. Sean knew all he could do was try and charm them, which isn't going to work on these guys. There was a pause when the four guys looked at each other and then at the big guy, begging him, *"Chino, let's get Ian into his room and clean him up. He needs his money more than we do."* Another one said, *"We need to watch out for him, he is one of us."*

You could see that Chino was upset and stormed away. They picked Ian up and carried him to the room, took him in, and cleaned him up before put him to bed. One of the guys came over to me and said, *"Not everyone here is an asshole, most of the people here are either addicts or have mental issues. I can relate with Ian because I also struggle with PTSD but not as bad as him. I go to V.A. for some help, but I, too, have been lost in the shuffle. As for Chino, he is all mouth. "* While they took Ian into his room and cleaned him up, I ran his credit card, and by George, it went through a $6.75 fare. Man, what I'll do for a buck. Leaving the motel, I felt good about avoiding a potentially dangerous situation. I got a rush looking down in the rabbit hole and found another personality to use. I was growing and learning to use each character for the right situation. Sometimes, you do need force and bravado, but other times, diplomacy and cool thinking works, and of course, you can't go wrong with humor. Denzel's plan worked, but I am curious to see what else he has to offer.

Chapter Four

During a 12-hour Taxi shift, there maybe 2 to 3 hours of shuttling people here to there. This left a lot of time on your hands to fill. You can drive to a location that you feel has the best paying customers, but other cabbies also know this is the ideal neighborhood. So, there maybe 6 or 7 taxies in a square mile and when you enter the area, the computer places you last in line. As I said before, when a fare is taken, you move up the list. Sometimes you could wait an hour for a ride, and the passenger is going down to the store, but you are playing the odds. There could be a passenger that wants to go to the airport, and that's an easy $60.

One of my favorite things to pass the time is to watch people. At night, you can see all types of people downtown. Homeless people, drunks, and druggies frequently come up to me asking for a handout. Each of them have a story to tell. The story of 'my car is broken down, and my wife and kids are waiting for me is the most popular one. If the homeless people look worse, I usually help them out. However, the drunks are a different story. I have them play my game. The one who tells the best story with great passion or does something entertaining will get a few dollars from me. You have to understand, I am a blink of the eye away from being on the street myself – joining this band of merry individuals.

Around 9:30, I was downtown, ready to head back to the barn, when I noticed a small black man in his sixties across the street. He caught my eye and started walking towards me. He's strutting across the road. I'm sure everyone has seen the type; hand in his crotch, and every other step is a little dip with his shoulders swaying side to side. He must have been something in his youth.

He taps on the window gesturing me to roll it down. I can smell the bad liquor and stale cigarettes. He says, *"Man, can you help a dude out? I need some money for a drink."* I liked that he didn't have a fancy story. He told it like it is, which I can appreciate. I asked for his name, and he slurred, *"Myron."*

"Myron, my name is Ed. You look like you were something years ago. What are you good at?"

His eyes lit up, and he shouted, *"DANCING."*

"Dancing Myron? Show me something good."

He walked over to the grass and grabbed a handful of sand (Florida has got a lot of sand), and proceeded to gently toss it on the street. As I am watching him, I can tell something special is about to happen. He was an artist in spreading out the sand. Myron stood up a little straighter as he prepared to perform. I get out of my taxi to get a better view.

Myron turns around and asks, *"What do you want to see?"*

"Do what you love. I'm sure it will be good."

He slowly walks over to the middle of the street, where

he has carefully prepared his stage and stood. Then, he murmured, *"1-2-3-4,"* and started a little soft shoe. It was very eloquent, I thought to myself. His arms were moving in a rhythm, and his shoes made that shuffling sound. It was fucking awesome! This is in the middle of a back street where the traffic was flowing. A car pulled up, and Myron just kept dancing. He had a smile spread across his face, he was in his own world. The car did not even hit the horn, they just got out to watch him dance.

I was into it so much that I stepped into his magic circle and started doing the moonwalk. I was pretty good at it. When my son was in fourth grade years ago, he called me at night (divorced) to see if I would come to his elementary school at 10 am and do the moonwalk during recess. He said none of his schoolmates believed I could do it. The next day I made a detour from work and did my thing in front of 30 kids. I got a standing ovation, well they were already standing. It was cool for my son to call me.

About 3 minutes in, a few more cars stopped, and more people got out. No horns, or noise, it was just a special place in time. Myron had his eyes closed when he started dancing. When he finished and opened his eyes, there were twenty people clapping for him. He just went up to the people and shook their hands. Everyone gave him money, and I noticed some fives, tens, and twenties. I also added to the bounty.

Eventually, the crowd broke up and went away. When

everyone was gone and out of sight, the smile washed off, and the life drowned out of his eyes like the eyes of the Terminator in the first movie. I wish I could tell you I had a conversation with him. That strut turned into a fast leap to the liquor store. I wondered what his story was, but I was not meant to know about the mystery dancer. All I know is that he was a performer tonight, and I was there to witness him in all his glory.

I don't always have drunks and crazy people, they simply happen to be the most interesting. Nobody wants to hear about me driving old ladies to the store and taking people to dinner. As a matter of fact, these are ninety percent of my fares. It's all I can do to stay awake. So, I decided to change that. Of all the movie characters, the best I do at the drop of a hat is Jerry Lewis in The Nutty Professor. I can nail his character, which is why I chuckled when the dentist tried to off himself a while back, and the doctor sounded like Jerry Lewis. Sometimes, I would do him at parties to get a few laughs. I went and bought some fake teeth and black reading glasses. This was around the time I decided to act as Jerry all day long. No strong personality, just an easy-going, funny character. I had never acted like him all day, so this should be fun.

When I said all day long, that is exactly what I meant. I woke up, put the teeth in, and wore the glasses. I went to check-in at the cab barn in character, knowing that I would get stares and all kinds of negative shit. I had to commit to the character and avoid letting anything deter me from my goal. It's funny because when I repaired those words out loud to myself, a calm came over me. I felt empowered and confident in a Jerry Lewis kind of way.

I was checking in, and of course, there were people staring at me. Instead of my normal tropical garb, I wore a nerdy striped shirt, bowtie, and no hat. One of the Haitians that I despised said, *"Hey, crazy man. Why are you dressed so stupid today?"* I replied in a melodic Nutty Professor voice, *"I have decided to relinquish my former personality, to better conform to my harsh surroundings."* Suffice to say, he had no idea what I said. He and his buddies just laughed, pointing their fingers towers me while they made some weird remark in Haitian. None of it bothered me because I had ammunition for any situation that may arise.

As the day wore on, I had different reactions. Most of the younger generation of people that had not seen the Nutty Professor just giggled under their breath. They smiled at me when I talked, unsure if I was putting them on. I was having a blast doing Jerry, it was stress-free. Then, of course, there were some people who had seen the classic movie.

I would open the door for them and say," *Hidee ho there. My name is Edward, and I ah am here to ah enhance your few minutes with me. If I can ah be of any assistance, please feel free ah to let me know."*

They caught on immediately and asked, *"Did anyone ever tell you that you look like and sound like...."*

I would interrupt them to exclaim, *"Jerry Lewis in The Nutty Professor."*

"YES"

"Yes, They do. I have no idea what they are ah talking about. I do not watch movies, and ah think all motion pictures are a waste of time." I loved it.

That is how most of the day went by until about 7 pm. I picked up a fine-looking gentleman in very classy garb and continued to stay in character, but he was unimpressed. The gentlemen asked, *"Could I rent your cab locally for one hour?"*

"Where locally?"

"I just want you to park at 33rd and 10th street." He explained.

I replied, *"I have been driving long enough to know that area at night on a Friday could be pretty dicey. I can't do it for anything less than 200 dollars, sir."*

He quickly responds, *"Done, other cabbies usually ask for 300."* This tells me that the place we are going to might be rough, and I need to stay on my toes. Damn, money will make you do stupid shit. He gave me an address on 10th street, and as I was getting close, there were a lot of cars in front of the house. Just as I was about to arrive, he instructed me, *"Turn off your lights and park under that big pine tree.*

We'll sit here for that hour."

A few minutes later, some young adults came out to the cab. I was looking at him in my rearview mirror, and no words were exchanged. In exchange for some money, he handed them something which I could not quite make out what it was, but I had a good guess. I am sitting there trying to stay in character with all these thoughts racing through my mind. I know he is selling drugs out of my cab. If he gets caught, am I an accomplice? Can I sit here and let him do this? Does he have a weapon? Clint is dying to turn around and confront him. Denzel is trying to figure out the best course of action, and Jerry is just sitting there sweating bullets.

I told myself I was going to stay in character all day, but this is tough. I decided to have Clint's attitude and Denzel's awareness of detail with my character. In my nutty voice, I asked, *"Excuse me, sir, I couldn't help but ah notice some sort of exchange with money involved. Could it be that you are selling drugs in the back seat of my vehicle?"* I was looking at him in the mirror and saw him turn to me, *"Do you have a problem with it? Other Cabbies are happy to make this kind of money."* "Yes, sir," I said with sweat pouring down my face and feeling the hairs on the back of my neck stand straight up. *"The money is quite substantial for the time involved in this sort of endeavor."* Instantly, my voice changed to Clint, *"But selling drugs does not sit well with me"* I was taking my false teeth out and putting on my other pair of glasses. Ed is really freaking out. It's the first time I felt uncomfortable with Clint taking the lead in a long time, and of course, I have no control.

Then, out of nowhere, something hit me in the back of the head. Stars were flying. I woke up with a crowd around me and people helping me to my feet. Naturally, the gentleman was gone, and the police were not called. I returned to the barn early. I was hurting bad, and there were no characters to confide in, just me. I knew Clint would eventually get me in trouble. Most of the time, I tried to put that danger in the back of my mind. The fact of the matter is that all those characters and maybe more will always be there, popping up whenever they want to.

The supervisor on duty at the barn wanted to know why my head was bloody. I told him to go fuck himself, Ed speaking. I turned in my keys and never went back. I stayed away from any situation that would bring Clint out. If someone yelled at me or I got into a heated discussion, I just left. I felt like The Incredible Hulk trying not to lose his temper and starting a shit storm.

It's been two weeks since I got hit in the head, and I haven't heard anything from the guys. Perhaps, avoiding the bad situations is probably the reason behind their disappearance. However, I needed to make some money, and the urge to look down that rabbit hole again was strong. I think I'll go for a drive.

Chapter Five

If I told anyone what was going on, I would be put away somewhere and never see daylight again. Consequently, I was on my own. We were still in recession, so as little as I wanted to, I went looking for a job and found one at another cab company who were glad to have me. This time, I was prepared with a different attitude and decided not to tell them about the other company. As I take my first fare, I am terrified. These movie characters believe they cannot be hurt, and I know sooner or later I will have to be in danger.

There are two things dominating my thoughts at this time were the possibility that the characters, especially Clint, can come out at any time. The more concerning thought is the fact that I like that feeling of being in harm's way. As I mentioned before, a major part of this job is waiting for a fare. This gives me a lot of time to think. I knew that driving again would definitely put me in worrying situations, and my body followed my character's irrational instincts. Eventually, I was going to break an arm, pull muscles, all sorts of things, especially at my old age. The other thing to worry about was Clint, who couldn't possibly keep getting this lucky when outbursts came. I had to address this.

There was something that I was not taking advantage of – a new ability to remember everything I read, saw, or experienced. I can read books in an hour and retain everything. Or, watch a YouTube video on how to play the guitar and start playing songs. I decided to learn Judo which uses the other person's weight against himself with little chance of straining my own body. I read several books on martial arts and took pieces of each discipline to develop my own style. I did it all with the intention of giving myself a chance to not only survive an encounter but to win unscathed.

I scoured through the internet for another part of my invisible armor and found a retractable nightstick that would do just fine. It can be kept in the pocket out of sight and, with a flick of the wrist, have a 3-foot weapon. I read about the use of this device and the Japanese art of Kendo which uses bamboo sticks in a defensive manner. I combined the two of these to develop a weapon. This defensive manner I came up with teaches discipline, just like Judo.

With my memory in full swing, I could learn more ways to protect myself, but these would suffice for the time being. I just wanted to be prepared if Clint came out of nowhere. I wanted to get back out there and earn some money. Another thing that was a byproduct of the bolt of lightning was my sensitive hearing. One night, after 2 fares, all of which I was in some sort of character, I heard a whimper. I stopped to listen and heard it again. It was coming from a wet and narrow alley. It was something I normally wouldn't have paid attention to, especially in a crappy neighborhood, but this night was different. As I listened closer, I could tell it sounded more like someone crying than a whimper. Now, as I sit there with all these different emotions flooding my brain, I am out trying to make money. Going down that alley will bring nothing but trouble, however, someone could be hurt. Then, I heard Clint say, *"Are you going to be a candy ass, or are you going to see if someone's hurt."* Normally, I would argue with him about all the dangers involved, but I agreed on this rare occasion, *"Yes, Yes I am, and I don't need you on my back about it."*

"Hey, Ed, my friend, you sound a little different, what's up?"

"I don't have time to explain," I said. *"Someone could be in trouble down that alley."*

It's true, I was a little different at present. My ongoing desire to go down the rabbit hole, my newfound abilities, and Clint in my head made me want to challenge myself and see what I was made of. Is this going to be the new me? I did not know, but I was going to take the first step and see.

I parked the cab near the alley, locked it up, and walked slowly down the alley. I reached in my pocket and took out the retractable nightstick, which I had named Blackie. I whipped it out to its full functioning length and held it with two hands In the Kendo attack position.

Who was this person inside me? It felt very comfortable, and there was no fear to be found. This was foolish, I said to myself. I've acquired a few new senses and learned some defensive moves, I shouldn't feel this good, but I did. I couldn't wait to see what was down this dark alley. I felt alive, my ears were tingling, whatever that meant, and I was aware of everything. I could smell the slight essence of perfume and taste cigarette smoke.

I was aware of my eyes adjusting to the dark alley as I scanned the area. I heard crying again, louder this time. It was a woman's cry. I came to a T in the alley, and the crying was coming from the left, I carefully peeked around the corner and saw a girl sitting on the street leaning up against the wall.

I was checking for all the possibilities. What was she doing back here? Is there anyone else around? Is she hurt? Too much thinking. Out of the corner of my eye, I saw the figure of a man with a knife. My Kendo training kicked in, and I whipped Blackie against his wrist. The knife went flying. Then a shot to his groin. As he was bending over a whack to the back of the head. He went down in slow motion with me instinctually turning to look for the girl. She was screaming at me, *"You're killing my boyfriend, you asshole!"* She picked up his knife came at me, to which I just slapped it out of her hand.

I said, *"Hey, I heard some crying in the alley and came back here to see if I could help."* She scurried over to the guy on the ground and put his head in her lap. *"We were just having an argument, and you came around the corner with that stick or whatever it is. Do you blame him for trying to protect me?"* I looked at the guy, and he was alright, and she went back to crying. I turned around and walked back to my cab. It was dark, and my body was still in this awareness mode, as it should be. Taking every precaution to make it back to my vehicle.

I was different. Reading books on self-defense, military strategies, Judo, and a jolt of electricity changed me. I returned to the cab and sat there mulling over what just happened when Clint popped up. *"So I see you're not a Candy ass anymore. What have you been up to?"* he said.

"Look, Big guy," I said, annoyed. *"You have been in my head through this transformation, and you know why I had to protect myself. The lightning bolt seems to have added a wrinkle. The strange thing is, I went down that alley looking to help someone. I also went down there looking for danger and an adrenaline rush. With your care-free-I-can't-die attitude and me starting to like it, it is just a matter of time before bad shit catches up to me."*

"I see your point," Clint said. *"Who do really think I am in your mind? I know you had many characters to get you through different situations in your life, but you practiced those voices and idiosyncrasies. I came out of nowhere. I came out when you needed to stand up for yourself, and yes, I put you through hell trying to get you to take on challenges for yourself. I never wanted to get you into trouble or cause*

harm, but I am your interpretation of Clint Eastwood from the movies and the fact you never really got hurt was pure luck. So what did you do? You recognized it and took the appropriate measures to protect yourself. I think I also appeared because deep down inside, you always wanted to go down the rabbit hole, but you also knew it would swallow your previous mind. The fact you got struck by lightning just sped up the learning process."

I sat there listening to myself in Clint's voice, and everything made sense. I never had a father figure to explain things and show me stuff, and I picked Clint of all the T.V. heroes to pick from, and I'm still here. *"So, Clint."* I said, *"Is this it. Have you taught me everything you know?"*

"No, it's not everything I know, but it is enough for you to move on from me. You have the other guys to help you out from time to time, and you will always be in character because you love to do it, not because you need to do it." Says Clint.

I sat there with a little panicking churn in my stomach when Clint said, *"Don't worry, my friend, you have come a long way. I will stay out of the way and let you learn, but I will be in the back of your mind, I'm not going to be too far, after all, I'm Clint Eastwood."*

I had a few more fares before it was time to head back to the barn. Ultimately, I clocked out and drove home. What a ride I've been on the last few months, it was exciting, but I wonder if I could really keep driving a cab. I'm still just making ends meet. On the other hand, I do have a photographic memory, self-confidence, and all my characters intact. I don't know what it is yet, but the world better watch out because we are coming.

Kerry Edwards

www.ingramcontent.com/pod-product-compliance
Lightning Source LLC
Chambersburg PA
CBHW051009050726
47592CB00007B/2769